What Others Are Saying About This Book

"This is the book of the century. We Declare should be required reading at every level of government. Yes, we have the power to spin the world into destruction, but even more important, we have the power to stop it. We Declare tells us how."
David B. – Veteran, Iraq and Afghanistan Wars

"I saw fighting every day. I saw helping every day. After reading your book, I realized what I had seen was an example of both parts of what a human being can do—or can be. It was exactly what the book points out and I saw it in real life. We are capable of more than what we give ourselves credit for. What could the world be like if we harnessed our helpful, visionary energy? Thanks for helping me make sense of the nonsense I experienced in war."
Leo Johnson – Veteran, Iraq War

"We Declare is real. It's honest. It tells it like it is. Everything is there—the tragedy and the hope. It's uplifting. I'm a career military guy and proud of it. I've read the book six times and passed it around. I thank you and my guys thank you!"
Leonard – Veteran, Gulf and Iraq Wars;
Orders pending for Afghanistan

"This book says it all. It looks everyone in the eye, asks the questions that need to be asked, judges no one, and challenges everyone."
Damon Bazzeghin – Veteran, Vietnam War

"You tell us not only what we become when we decide war is the answer, you also tell us how to keep peace at the forefront of our strategy. We don't seem to learn that peace is a better answer than war. I wish I could send a copy to every head of state around the world!"

Mark – Veteran, Afghanistan War; two tours—so far

"You tell it like it is in the first half—and how it could be in the second half. I really like the way you set a direction for the promise of what's inside us already. It's not prescriptive about what to do—it's enlightening and inspirational, and individuals can see the myriad possibilities of what they could do."

David Bressem – Veteran, Vietnam War

"This book makes it clear that no matter what we are capable of in our worst minds, we are capable of the glorious in our best minds. Big or small, so long as our actions come from the heart of human connection, we are better for it, contribute more to those around us, and set a different example for the next generations. When you stop seeing enemies everywhere you look, it makes life better for everyone. And thanks for saving my life and taking such good care of me back then."

Eugene Brice – Veteran, Vietnam War
(and former patient of Penny's)

"As usual, you don't mince words—you just capture the human spirit and hold it up for all to see. You ask the best of us and understand and forgive the worst."

Maureen Lynch

"What you did over there, and how you set the stage for what is still possible if we take our blinders off and set our opinions aside—even after all these years—is inspiring. You have an unwavering eye for seeing what is and what could be—and the individual responsibility required. And the poetry brings it alive. It's impossible not to feel the roller coaster of human emotion."

Paula Cox – Journalist

"Wow! The first part is cold water in the face. The second part is the energy of compassion. No holds barred and not a wasted word."

Jerry L. – Veteran, Iraq and Afghanistan Wars

"I honestly never thought about all that goes into the decisions and planning for war. I just got called up and did my job. I never thought about a decision for war and a decision for peace and what those actions entail. I made it back minus an eye and a foot. I wish I had your books back then. I've come to terms with what I did to others and what others did to me—but the world view just got bigger after reading your words. A more purposeful way of living just got clearer. Thanks!"

Barry Horten – Veteran, Vietnam War

"I did my duty in Iraq and Afghanistan and even though I did my job the best I could, there always seemed to be something missing. What was I offering beyond destruction? I didn't second guess what was required and I did what I had to do, but there's even more I can do now and on a much broader level. You just helped me decide what that is. Bless you Ms. Rock."

Chuck R. – Veteran, Iraq and Afghanistan Wars

"Your books have had the single biggest impact on my life. I chose a profession to be helpful to others so they could bury their demons. Meeting you and reading your work, I now realize that burial is not as effective as looking them straight in the eye.

We Declare let me see the danger is living from the limitations of being judgmental. The gift is calling upon and living from what's best in us. I hope my new understanding will benefit my patients as much as it has changed my life."

Linda C. – Clinical Psychologist

We Declare

We Declare

The Truth About War
and our Responsibility For Peace

Penny Rock

Penny Rock • Woodside, California

We Declare
The Truth About War
and our Responsibility For Peace

By Penny Rock

Other works by Penny Rock:
CDs
Power of a Clear Mind: Keep Your Bearings in Any Circumstance
The 8 Essential Ingredients of Healing: From Anything, Anywhere,
    Anytime
Books
He Called Me Lieutenant Angel: A Love Song From War
We Declare: The Truth About War and our Responsibility for Peace
Available at www.powerofaclearmind.com

Published by: Penny Rock
www.powerofaclearmind.com

ISBN 978-0-9787156-2-5

First Printing 2006
Second Printing 2008, revised
Third Printing 2010
Fourth Printing 2011, revised

Printed in the United States of America
Cover Design by JD Buckwell
Author Photo by Terry Gardner
Vietnam Photos courtesy of Penny Rock

*For all who are dedicated to
creating a future that
respects and celebrates
the potential of
unified humanity
living the dream of peace.*

CONTENTS

Introduction 13

The Truth About War 17

Where Do Soldiers Come From? 24

Preparing for War 26

Fit to Kill 29

One and Twenty 30

Capital Expenditure 32

Foxhole Buddy 33

Fatigue 34

Hometown Girl 36

Hide the Dead and Wounded 38

Don't Look Away 39

Blue Dress 40

Nightsounds 43

A Little Touch of War 45

Before the War 46

Relentless 48

Nurses Don't Cry 50

Body Counts are Irrelevant 51

Red Blood — Black Gold 53

Euphemisms of War 55

The Last Person 57

What Will Become of Us? 59

Our Responsibility for Peace   **61**

Live for Your Country   66

Kitchen Table   67

What Price Truce   68

We Declare   69

Enemy Friend   70

Peace Full   72

Time is of the Essence   73

I Learned About Living   74

Time Slowly Passes   77

Our Purpose is to Love Each Other   78

Viet Nam Counsel   79

The Risk of Peace   81

Peace Is   82

Precious Peace   83

Courage   84

Going Back Again   85

Could You Really Have a War?   87

Constant Spirit   88

What Was Your Intention?   89

One Among the Many   90

Give My Love to the World   92

Embarking on the Path of Peace   **93**

About the Author   **104**

INTRODUCTION

I was an Army Nurse stationed in Vietnam during the period of the Tet Offensive. All of us with wartime experience have seen too much. Too much death. Too much destruction. Too much carnage. We also saw not enough. Not enough lives saved. Not enough respect. Not enough truth.

So, how do you deal with all that is "too much" and "not enough?" How do you make sense of the nonsensical? My way of dealing with the insanity of war was to write. I wrote about what I saw and felt. I wrote prose and poetry to put words to life in the midst of death. And I wrote secretly. I shared none of what I wrote with others. My words were privileged communications between my mind and my heart.

After returning to the United States, I thought it was important to speak the truth about what war requires of, and does to, those who are in the midst of it. My desire to share what I had learned was not enough to elicit attention, reflection, or action from those not otherwise engaged in some form of protest. Even many engaged in protest saw us as traitorous for having been in the war regardless of the need for our skills or our personal positions on the war.

I found there was precious little interest in what I, or any of us, had to say. I stopped speaking. I stopped writing. I couldn't stop remembering.

Several years ago, I entered another war, called cancer. After once again facing death and going through all the necessary treatment to keep it at bay, the spigot of words was once again turned on full blast. And the first subject I wrote about was war.

I've never written for the purpose of being published. I initially shared some of my work with a small circle of family and friends. They said I should publish. They said the work was inspirational and relevant to the current world situation. But what did they know? They were my personal supporters, so they were probably prejudiced.

When I began sharing the work publicly, others said the same things and wanted to buy my books. Ooops! All I had were my three-ring binders. And besides, what did they know? They were probably predisposed to like, or be curious about, my kind of writing. They were potential supporters, so they were probably prejudiced.

I was busy writing and loving every minute of it. I was also busy not listening to the advice of those who seemed to think it was sensible to publish. But, one thing caught my attention: the similarity of their comments, and their persistence about their belief that sharing my message might be helpful to people.

I have always believed my purpose in life is to create a higher consciousness in the world as a global voice for healing and peace. I don't mean that to sound lofty or arrogant. I don't mean I need to travel all over the world spreading my ideas. My purpose has simply given me a litmus test from which to live my life. It's not a bumper sticker. It's a thought I hold close to my heart. In fact, I've never before put these words in print for others to see.

It finally occurred to me that words meant to inform, enlighten, and inspire are meant to be read and heard. Not forced on people, but available for the moment when eyes are ready to see and ears are ready to hear.

In times of global uncertainty, rigidity, judgment, self-indulgence, and manipulation of societal fear, it is all the more important we step forward with a message of hope and possibility. And now is such a time. Now is the time to recognize we are the message we send. We are collectively and individually culpable for previous paths of destruction, and we are equally capable of paving pathways to peace. But only if we are willing to use our "voices" to articulate the vision of an enlightened society where peace is the norm and we are the stewards who preserve and protect this treasure.

We have no control over the thoughts and actions of others, but we do have the responsibility to voice our views and to listen openly and respectfully to those of others.

And, if I know nothing else, I do know this: platitudes of peace are not sufficient or even admirable. We cannot begin to entertain visions of peace until we are willing to look at the human face and consequences of war and understand the collective state of mind that placed us there.

So, I still write for myself, but I'm willing to share my message with anyone interested in hearing regardless of their concurrence with what they perceive the message to be. If what I have to say, and how I say it, provides assistance or relief to others, I am honored, grateful, and humbled.

I have selected a few of my poems that describe my views about the truth of war, and others that beckon us to consider our role in the creation and preservation of peace. These poems are the children of my heart and I hope they treat you kindly.

THE TRUTH ABOUT WAR

A hospital alone shows what war is.

Erich Maria Remarque

THE TRUTH ABOUT WAR

Has someone ever said to you, "Forget about the past. It's over and you can't do anything about it."? It sounds like good advice because it's housed in a true statement. This bit of pop wisdom would mean we should forget about the moment we understood the principles of math, the birth of a baby, or how to drive a car.

Since the past is housed in our memory, we would have to wipe that slate clean continually. Of course, it's impossible because the creation of our past is always a nanosecond behind us. So, what does the advice really mean?

It usually refers to those experiences we deem unpleasant or painful, such as a divorce, illness, or job loss. But, have you ever had a painful experience that you now view to be a blessing? Have you ever been grateful for an experience because you learned a valuable lesson regardless of how painful it was?

Our past consists of previous experience. Memory is the storage facility for our past. Like any other storage facility, the past is available to be viewed throughout our lives. As our perspective changes, so does our relationship with the past. Without the past or the memory to store it, we would be unable to learn. And learning is always the blessing.

This is why we must remember and speak the truth about war. If we choose to ignore or avoid looking at the consequences of war, we are destined to repeat them eternally.

War provides no useful benefit to the world. Some would argue that there are technological and medical advancements that occur as a result of war. The artificial and arbitrary need produced by war requires that we experiment on the people placed in harm's way, ours and theirs. Could we not spend money for necessary research, development, and experimentation without a war?

War diminishes us as human beings and as nations. War should be the last option and only for the purpose of self-defense from invasion, to be good global citizens by aiding others to protect human rights, or to nurture and stabilize international movements toward democracy. War is not an accident. We plan, prepare, and decide to declare war. We are the provocateurs and perpetrators. We have ourselves to hold accountable for its blight upon the human spirit and dignity.

We are also the ones who can look at our past with a clear mind and assess what got us into the fray in the first place. I'm not talking about placing blame. There's a never-ending supply of that commodity and it is the quality that motivates us to find or create enemies in the first place. A mindset of lying, bickering, hate, and anger is not the place where peaceful action can begin. It is not the place where visions can be born.

I am talking about our ability to look nonjudgmentally at the human face of war.

When we do, the truth of its folly becomes readily apparent. And only then can we learn the lessons necessary to create a world where annihilation of each other is considered barbaric, uncivilized, and unthinkable.

Thank You for Your Service. Welcome Home.

Lovely words, aren't they? I have no doubt they are sincerely meant in the moment, but what do they really mean? More and more, they sound like a pro forma mantra. The proper thing to say. The more I hear about the disturbing and inevitable effects of war, I have the uneasy sense there is an expiration date looming over the heads of our current vets. An expectation they should take a couple of months to rest and heal, and then "get back to normal." I have an uneasy sense of déjà vu. I hope I am terribly wrong.

As common as these statements are today, they were absent from the national vocabulary upon our return from Vietnam.

Returning vets were given to understand they were unwelcome in the midst of a country that had grown weary of the TV war. They should get back on track with their lives, get back to normal, and "get over it," "it" being their experiences in war. They should engage in normal conversation and take a sleeping pill for their nightmares. They should suck it up, see a shrink if necessary but don't let anyone know. It made them look weak and reflected poorly on the family. And, above all, they should not talk about the war! The conspiracy of silence grew deep roots. Another version of "Don't ask. Don't tell."

In the war zone, we had little ability to learn about what was happening "in country" or elsewhere in the world. We didn't have the Internet or cell phones to learn about world events, talk to friends and family, or to share our stories and express our views.

When I think back to that time, and the increasingly pervasive psychologically claustrophobic feeling, it's easy to see why many of us chose to shut our mouths and lay down our pens.

I can't speak for others, but I realize that because of my decision to maintain silence for so long, I did little to serve my vision of peace. I didn't curl up in a ball. I've lived an active and engaged life—a life dedicated to hope, healing, and peace. But there were words I could and should have spoken, and I could and should have shared my writing. And I felt the burden of guilt and shame for not doing so.

Today, I see things more clearly.

Pointing fingers keeps us from the real task. We all are accountable for what we've done—or not done. It ultimately doesn't matter how we got to war. We need to focus on how to get to peace.

War is not an accident. We plan, prepare for, and declare it. It comes from a state of mind that harbors fear and suspicion. Those feelings may even be well founded. But, it should be the last resort rather than the first reaction.

Peace is not an accident either. We aspire to a journey of respectful co-existence on our planet. And the aspiration is more important than any imagined end state because it fuels the collective forward movement. Aspiration binds unlikely comrades together in the joint responsibility for protecting and preserving the pathway of peace.

———◆———

Our lives begin to end the day we become silent about things that matter.

Dr. Martin Luther King, Jr.

WHERE DO SOLDIERS COME FROM

Where do soldiers come from?
Are they born or are they made?
Do they know the role will change them,
That they'll never be the same?

Do we teach them how to kill
People they don't know?
Do we teach them how to die
Before they have a chance to grow?

Dinner tables in dining rooms
Filled with conversation.

Parks filled with strollers
The infant cargo still asleep.

Parlors with ice cream cones and sundaes,
And sodas being shared.

Swirling on the dancefloor
And singing in the Sunday choir.

Playing children run and fall,
Then help each other up.

Young boys, young girls
Nervous in their first embrace.

Weekend nights without a care
Driving cars with revving engines.

Tiny hands and tiny feet
Getting tangled in the crib.

Schoolrooms filled with books,
And clouds of dust from chalk erasers.

Football games with marching bands,
Beaches with romping dogs and castles made of sand.

Looking at the stars on a brilliant moonlit night,
And dreaming dreams of who to be.

That's where soldiers come from.

PREPARING FOR WAR

It's not a simple thing,
Preparing for a war.
Supplies are too numerous to mention
For the aftermath of blood and gore.

Have you given any thought
To the macabre list of needs?
They're ordered for the children
Who die for adult sins and deeds.

War isn't a backyard child's game.
Death's not signified by a playful punch.
You can't send them out to fight,
Then call them home for lunch.

The supplies needed are consumables.
Inventory anticipates need.
Those customers would have been our future.
Now they lie upon the ground and bleed.

Have you thought about what's needed for a war?
Perhaps you'll benefit from instruction.
Here's a little sample of what's required
When you embark on youth's destruction.

Of course there is a need
For artillery by the tons.
Trucks, and tanks, and ambulances,
And ammunition for the guns.

Helmets and uniforms of camouflage
That don't disguise the human form.
Radios, rockets, mortars, grenades
And choppers and bombers are the norm.

Journalists and photographers will be mobilized
To chronicle the story of the war.
Some will do it with integrity.
Some will be buzzards to the gore.

Do you feel prepared now for a war?
Do you have all you need for winning?
I've so much more to tell you.
That was only the beginning.

One Hundred Thousand High School Boys to be
Sacrificed as fodder.
Renewal orders for several hundred thousand more.
Prosthetic devices for all limbs.
Extra skin from a bank for grafting.
Crutches for the lucky.
Wheelchairs for those who aren't.
Glass eyes to spare the sensitivities of others.
Bags of blood and platelets.
Dog Tags –two each to identify you when you're dead.
Food rations that may be edible.
Medications for disease indigenous to the host country…
"Host" being a euphemism.
Medications for pain, infection, blood volume,
And hydration.
Special ointments for burning flesh…
That won't stop burning.
Thousands of medical personnel inducted.
IV bags, poles, needles, and tubes.

Enough dressings and bandages to swaddle the earth.
Myriad tubes to insert in every orifice...
Natural or manmade.
Bottles to collect the drainage that
Courses through the tubes.
Medical equipment from surgical instruments to
Respirators to heart pumps.
Coffins ordered to meet the need for increased volume.
Stone engravers notified so inventory can be enlarged.
Standard letters drafted to notify families of their loss.

You'll need to order body-bags.
No need to be concerned with size.
Don't worry about the color.
It's just a cloak to shroud demise.

You'll need the largest airplanes
For shipping home the dead.
Don't forget to strip search them.
Words of objection won't be said.

Has the payment of their lives
Finally settled our shameful debt?
Be careful what you prepare for.
We haven't learned our lesson yet.

FIT TO KILL

Your body's been examined
And determined fit to kill.
They neglected to inform you,
You're just as likely to be killed.

They say that you're a man now
And can kill for God and country.
What place must your mind enter
To kill another body?

What thoughts do you encounter
When staring down their barrel?
They too have been examined
And determined fit to kill.

To do this to our children
Is our collective shame.
We never learn our lesson,
It's our collective blame.

But, war is pure and noble,
Young men must take their places.
So what if thousands die?
There are thousands more new faces.

The pride within your mother
To know she bore you for this fate.
The joy within your father
To refer to you as "late".

But, your body's been examined,
And determined fit to kill.
They neglected to inform you,
You're just as likely to be killed.

ONE AND TWENTY

I am but one and twenty.
I live in a land called war.
Death is all around me.
I never knew such pain before.

Clocks tick hours and minutes.
Calendar pages turn.
They mark the passage of my life.
A life that others spurn.

I am so very young.
It's very likely I am told,
I'll need to give my life
Before I can grow old.

They say it's not uncommon
For people of my youth
To be sacrificed for country.
I fear it is the truth.

I'm told I have one purpose.
My job is just to give.
It may require that I die
So someone else may live.

I must deny my heart.
I must not love or grieve.
I can only weep goodbye
As youthful bodies leave.

So many bodies through my hands.
I cannot count the number.
I just feel the terrible burden
As I send them to death's slumber.

I feel so alone here,
No love and no affection.
The only thing my country gives me
Is lies and misdirection.

There appears to be no future.
My life ends here it seems.
The war has stopped me in my tracks,
And silenced all my dreams.

It doesn't make much sense to me.
I was born, but for what reason?
To extinguish life in the bloom of youth
Is a cowardly act of treason.

I am but one and twenty.
I live in a land called war.
I see life through veils of tears.
I want to live and nothing more.

CAPITAL EXPENDITURE

To feed our hungry egos
We try to buy control of other's fate.
Then to our great surprise,
All we've really purchased
Is their undying hate.

We invade their land, and wage a war,
And then proclaim our might.
We flex our righteous muscles
Of imperial arrogance,
Then send our youth to fight.

To subsidize the great adventure
We spend young lives in haste.
We incur a debt impossible to repay
When Human Capital
Is the currency we waste.

FOXHOLE BUDDY

Until death do us part.
Others think this is a marriage vow.
But for us it's an unspoken vow in war.
We sign the contract with our eyes
As we look into each other's soul.

The bond is not created out of passion,
But by fear and need.
We have no history and an uncertain future.
We may have only met this morning,
But we commit to each other forever.
Forever might be tonight.

I'll stay awake so you can rest.
You'll give me food to keep my strength.
I'll walk ahead to show you the path.
You'll hold the light so I can see.
I'll take the bullet so you can live.
You'll cover my face to show respect.

We are foxhole buddies tied to each other
By endless trust and bottomless faith.
Ours is a bargain sealed in blood.
We will live for each other
Until death do us part.

FATIGUE

Fatigue is a state of body.
It's been a month of the never-ending parade of bodies.
Some alive, some just barely, some with the vacant
eyes of death. You've never been so tired
and your body rebels against what it is called upon to do.
You yearn for hours and hours of dreamless sleep.
Your body sags with the heaviness of fatigue.

Fatigue is a state of mind.
It's been two months of the parade of bodies.
You marvel at the body's resilience. You wonder if
the people inside them have the same strength.
You reel at the impossible injuries inflicted in war.
You couldn't dream up these sights.
But, you do...in your nightmares.
Your mind begins to numb to protect you
from what you can't bear.
Your mind sags with the heaviness of fatigue.

Fatigue is a state of spirit.
It's been three months of the parade of bodies.
You know now it will never end.
Sometimes you wonder if it's the same people
over and over. It seems impossible
there could be so many different ones.
But, then you know the answer.
There is an eternal supply of bodies.
Your spirit sags with the heaviness of fatigue.

Fatigue is a kind of uniform.
Its drab colors of earth are meant to let you blend
into your surroundings. It's called protective cover.
But it doesn't protect you from dying.
It's been four months of the parade of bodies and
they have indeed blended into their surroundings...
some permanently.
The red of blood, green of bile, yellow of pus, and
pasty white and gray of dying flesh.
All these glorious colors blend with the earth.
They leave part or all of themselves behind.
The uniform of fatigue, the protective cover,
has captured your body, your mind, and your spirit.
And now you sag with the heaviness of death.

HOMETOWN GIRL

I'm a hometown girl
Suddenly gone to war.
Forgotten by my people,
I'm not remembered anymore.

Women don't interest the press.
They don't believe we're here.
And even if a few exist,
There's nothing for us to fear.

It's not like we're in danger.
We're not near enemy lines.
We're nowhere near the action.
We're not near enemy mines.

We're safe from grenades and mortars.
No snipers are around us.
We're safe from guns and rockets.
No enemy surrounds us.

They have no clue
What we see and do.
They have no clue
What's false or true.

Do they think we're handing out aspirin?
Do they think we're handing out water?
Don't they know we're not on vacation?
Don't they know we deal in slaughter?

If they could see the carnage
That's always before my eyes.
If they could see the remnants
Of a boy before he dies.

If their skin dripped in bloody stain,
If their hands wiped off shards of brain,
If they could see boys freshly slain,
They'd see how lives are lost in vain.

Our bodies are covered in blood,
And pus, and urine, and guts.
We're drenched in bodily fluids.
Back home they're calling us sluts.

Women live in the middle of war.
There are no secure or safe places.
It's a crime to deny our existence.
It's a crime to cover our faces.

If they're asked for the real story,
It's easier to resist.
It's safer to ignore us
And deny that we exist.

What fantasy world do they live in?
Do they think that war is pristine?
Ignoring the blood we bathe in,
Won't keep their conscience clean.

HIDE THE DEAD AND WOUNDED

Hide the dead and wounded.
Keep them hidden from our sight.
Let's keep our dirty little secret.
Send them home in dead of night.

If we stay arm's length from evidence,
We don't deal with war's brutality.
With no photos to disturb us,
We keep distance from reality.

They're expected to die bravely,
Yet we've no courage to look.
Perhaps if we did,
We'd close war's vicious book.

DON'T LOOK AWAY

If you want to wage a war,
Don't resort to euphemisms,
Just call it by its name.
It's not a skirmish or a conflict,
An unpleasantness or game.

If you want to support a war,
Then look it in the face.
Remember all the loss of life
Is part of your disgrace.

You can't avoid the consequences.
You need to see them.
You need to look them in the eye.
Mutilated bodies with empty, glassy stare.
That's how it looks when youth is forced to die.

There are sounds that you must hear,
The cries and screams of death.
The loudest sound is deafening silence
After their last breath.

To look at what you have destroyed
Requires courage and humility,
Decency, and respect.
And you must admit to your participation
And own up to its effect.

You can't look away from atrocities,
Or ignore the waste of lives unfinished.
Your choice to engage in legal massacre
Renders all humanity diminished.

BLUE DRESS

I have a blue dress.
It's perfect for dances.
I can tell that he likes it.
I can tell by his glances.

We slip into town
For a little diversion
To escape for awhile
War's total immersion.

We dine and we dance,
We kiss and we talk.
Before it's too late,
We take a short walk.

He loves my blue dress,
Says it matches my eyes.
Then he tells me he loves me
Under warm, moonlit skies.

We head back to the compound.
It's a rather long trip.
As we approach the MP's,
I feel fear's viselike grip.

I have a blue dress,
But there'll be no more dancing.
We're under attack,
So there'll be no romancing.

The night has turned ugly.
We hear war's booming sound.
Before we can run,
We're both blown to the ground.

I feel his body
Draped over my own.
I see his guts spilling.
I see a bare bone.

My love has been wounded.
His blood soaks my dress.
I know he won't make it.
He's in mortal distress.

I drag him to surgery
Where doctors will cut,
And try to repair
His poor shattered gut.

The doctors are sorry.
They did all they could.
They move to the next boy,
Just as they should.

My love lies in his bed
Still covered in grime.
His heartbeat is thready.
It's a matter of time.

I have a blue dress,
As blue as my eyes.
I wear it while waiting
As he slowly dies.

I cover his body
And stand by his bed.
The last time I'll see him
Is now…and he's dead.

I remove the bloody blue dress.
It's lost all its beauty.
So I put on a scrub dress,
And get back to duty.

I had a blue dress.
It wasn't worn often.
I just sent it with him
To be placed in his coffin.

NIGHTSOUNDS

Dusk sneaks up beside me…goosebumps on my skin.
Night falls.
Lights dim.
I hope I will drift into the quiet,
Dreamless sleep of a child.
I am a child. But sleep escapes my fragile grasp.
Awake or asleep, I'm visited by
Ever-present nightsounds.

Metal pans and cabinet doors. Charts shoved into racks.
Beds crash through the doors, and bed rails
Lock us inside our wartime cribs.
IV bottles clink together as though they
Toast our health…or impending death.
Drainage bottles emptied, liquid sloshes and tries to
Wash away the evidence of crime.
Chairs scrape along the floor…then footsteps in a hurry.
Retching, moans, and crying out from fear.
Those are the nightsounds that I hear.

The steady drone of voices like the backbeat of a song.
Nurses giving orders.
Corpsmen asking questions.
Patients wanting answers.
Human sounds of despair.
Muffled sobs, cries of fear, calling out names.
Shouting at the enemy or to our buddies for some help.
Breathing that is labored and the
Rhythmic respirator's sigh.
Struggling in bed, fighting the unseen enemy
In our own private war.

In the background, the sounds of war that put us here.
Guns and bombs and mortars.
Rockets and grenades.
I hear my own heart beating…I wonder for how long.
This symphony around me…this orchestra of war…
Plays music of destruction. Sounds I know too well.
The ever-present nightsounds…
My own glimpse into hell.

A LITTLE TOUCH OF WAR

A bit of you, a bit of me
A bit of them and more.
We're all just little morsels
On the smorgasbord of war.

Everyone is mixed together
Like ingredients in a stew.
It's hard to tell the different flavors.
I'll just hope it isn't you.

Who'll ever know we went to war
If you never really call it one?
Just call it a small conflict,
And tidy up when you are done.

We only want a little war,
A sip, a dash, a smidge, a drop.
And when we've tasted just a bit of blood
We'll tell the war to stop.

Just treat it like a virus.
Just let it run its course.
And when enough of youth are dead,
We'll offer some remorse.

We all just want a clean war
Without the dirt and grime.
In the safety of TV screens,
We keep our distance from the crime.

BEFORE THE WAR

I wonder what's the matter with him.
He's not the way he was before.
He's not the way he used to be.
The way he was before the war.

He had no way of knowing
What horrors were in store.
Then communication ceased
When he went off to war.

He left while only in his teens.
Now he's so much older.
The warmth of his youth is gone.
His spirit's so much colder.

His eyes look deeply haunted.
He has no joy anymore.
He doesn't laugh and rarely smiles.
He stares down at the floor.

He speaks in cryptic code.
He talks of blood and gore.
Then lapses into silence,
Since he came back from war.

I wonder what he saw there
That fills his eyes with fright.
All those unknown terrors
Keep him awake at night.

Certain sounds will startle him
And send him out the door.
Will he ever have peace again,
As he had before the war?

He turns away from mirrors.
Who he sees must frighten him.
There's no respite in his mind
Because all his thoughts are grim.

I don't know what to say to him.
I can't talk as I did before.
He's not the person that I knew
Before he went to war.

He doesn't even look the same,
So pale and so thin.
It's like another person
Came back inside his skin.

He used to be such fun.
So easy to adore.
It's like he disappeared
When he returned from war.

I wonder what became of him.
I never see him anymore.
He's not the person he once was.
I mean, before the war.

RELENTLESS

Relentless onslaught.
Relentless assault.
Relentless attack
That isn't our fault.

There's no intermission.
There's no short reprieve.
New bodies arrive,
As old bodies leave.

Does anyone care
How we spend our time?
The squandering of life
Is our country's crime.

Do they think war's romantic?
Do they think there's allure?
I'll try to describe
The life we endure.

Truckloads of bodies stacked on each other.
Grotesque gaping wounds.
Muscle and bowel hanging loose.
Limbs crudely severed…heads too.
Puddles, and rivers,
And fountains, and geysers of blood.
Eyes gone or hanging out of sockets.
Faces gone…not just mashed…gone.
Maggots in the wounds.
Worms in the esophagus and colon.
Bloated bodies…victims of burns.
Charred skin falls off in our hands.
Vegetative states from head wounds.
Paralysis from severed spines.

No limbs left…at all.
Putrid smells of infection, pus,
decomposing flesh, burned
bodies, explosives, charcoal fires,
and garbage piled high in our streets.
Sounds of war on Full Volume
All day, all night, every day.
Snipers use us for target practice.

Letters from home
Assuming we've been sightseeing
And aren't in any danger.
Newspaper articles
Berating us for being here,
As if we had declared the war.
Bodies dying, toe tags in place,
A sheet over the face,
And finally, body bags
Stacked like cordwood.
Frightened. No sleep.
Yet we need to be sharp for the patients.
Bodies lying everywhere waiting to be treated.
Running out of operating rooms and beds.

And that's just a little sample
Of an average day.

There's no turning back.
It's here we must stay.
We've no power to send,
The demons away.

The horrors we live with,
Are too painful to say.
The horrors will haunt us,
'Til our dying day.

NURSES DON'T CRY

There's something in our code
That says we must be strong.
The experts say we don't feel.
The experts would be wrong.

Nurses handle anything.
Nurses never fear.
Nurses keep emotions buttoned,
And never shed a tear.

We're bathed in daily suffering,
Every scream and every moan.
Nurses hearts aren't empty,
Or cold as marble stone.

Nurses must keep distance from their patients;
Brains and feelings kept apart.
How could we live through our daily Hell,
And not have a broken heart?
Of course our hearts are broken
By the patients that we tend.
And every time we allow the tears,
We fear they'll never end.

Nurses are invisible.
We're lonely to the bone.
And when we find the time to cry,
We cry our tears alone.

BODY COUNTS ARE IRRELEVANT

If body count doesn't matter,
If it's not relevant who dies,
Then your words of wanting peace
Are just a pack of cruel lies.

Uniforms signify the difference
Between soldiers and civilians.
But weapons of mass destruction
Are efficient killing millions.

If you think that war's romantic,
If you think that war is thrilling,
Then don your gear and point your gun.
You'll find enjoyment in the killing.

Being killed is the luck of the draw.
Nothing about it is exotic.
It depends on who you're standing next to.
Being killed is just quixotic.

Not counting enemy dead is so convenient.
It gives them anonymity.
They're rendered inconsequential and faceless.
An illusion sustained through infinity.

It's a nifty way to pretend
No blood's on our national hands.
It's open season on our enemy.
Just don't document where he lands.

Of course it's a shame if our boys die.
They come from the land of "good".
How value of life depends on country of origin
Is something I've never understood.

If we tabulate what we have done,
An accounting's hard to resist.
If we don't count them in the first place,
It's as if they didn't exist.

RED BLOOD – BLACK GOLD

I remember a land so long ago.
A land where dirt was red.
A time when goals were a mystery.
Hard to believe what government said.

But we knew we weren't fighting for rice.
Our country had plenty of that.
Our way of life wasn't dependent upon
What their poor land begat.

Now we're in a new war,
With goals equally shrouded in gauze.
But this time, we have a dependence.
This time, we have a cause.

The official reason keeps changing
To suit political need.
But the effect is entirely predictable.
Our people and theirs will bleed.

Something deep in their earth
Produces precious oil.
Our country greedily covets
What's buried in their soil.

So we march in
To strip them bare,
So we can consume
More than our share.

Boys and girls open their veins
To dutifully shed their blood.
It soaks into the dirt
And mixes with oily black mud.

Our leaders are fearless.
They're arrogant and bold.
Who cares if Red Blood
Is spilled for Black Gold?

What's the price of a gallon
Of shiny, black crude?
Spending gallons of blood
Is more than just rude.

The geysers erupt
Spewing red tinged black mud.
Is the price of the oil
Worth the price of the blood?

How would you feel
If you'd just been told,
That your child's Red Blood
Was siphoned for Black Gold?

EUPHEMISIMS OF WAR

Not having courage to call something
By it's ugly proper name,
Doesn't make it beautiful,
Or change the source of blame.

"Conflict, skirmish, battle, unpleasantness".
Sounds like inconvenient upset in the day.
Like children scuffling on the playground,
And getting in each other's way.

Blood was "spilled" upon the battlefield.
That's an interesting thing to be said.
As though their veins accidentally overflowed,
So now, they're accidentally dead.

They "lost" their limbs in battle.
They "lost" their ears and eyes.
It's doubtful they just misplaced them,
Or we wouldn't hear such frightened cries.

He was killed by "friendly" fire.
It has a familial sound.
I wonder if he felt the warmth of friendship
As he lay dying on the ground.

"Morbidity and mortality",
Mean "wounded and dead".
"Fatally shot, mortally wounded",
Means their lives were shed.

These are euphemisms of war.
They change little with the times.
They can't change the consequences.
We're still accountable for our crimes.

Treading carefully with language
Won't guarantee they'll survive.
Not calling war a "war"
Won't keep the kids alive.

THE LAST PERSON

When you were a boy
And climbed up in the tree,
You must have had fun
Deciding what to be.

Doctor was "A".
Cowboy was "B".
Policeman was "C".
Soldier was "Z".

When you finished high school,
A letter came for thee.
A Draft Board invitation.
Did you think you could flee?

Then you went off to war,
And flew across the sea.
I'll bet you didn't know
You'd never again be free.

After the battle,
You came to me.
And now I'm debriding
The stump of your knee.

If you had a choice
About who would be
The last person in life
You'd ever see,
I doubt it would be me.

Your temperature's rising
To a dangerous degree.
Your life is soon ending.
Your doctors agree.

Now you've no choice
About who will be
The last person in life
You'll ever see.
I'm sorry…it will be me.

WHAT WILL BECOME OF US

What will become of us
When we at last return
To the land of our birth,
The land for which we yearn?

Surely they will welcome us
Saying thanks for jobs we didn't want.
They'll help us mourn our dead,
Our loss of youth and injured hope.

They'll listen to our stories
And understand their message.
They'll look at all our pictures,
And wipe our tears for what we saw.

They'll hold us in their arms
When nightmares pay a call.
They'll ask us to teach them lessons
And they'll learn what not to do.

They'll learn that war is loss
And love is gain.
They'll learn that sacrifice of youthful life
Is only filled with pain.

OUR RESPONSIBILITY
FOR PEACE

Peace cannot be achieved through violence; it can only be attained through understanding.

Albert Einstein

OUR RESPONSIBILITY FOR PEACE

Peace is not the absence of war or a state of truce. It is not a declaration or an accident. It is not the responsibility of others or a final destination. It is not beholden to a religion or an ideology. It is not a static condition or a vulnerable position.

Peace is a state of mind and a decision. It is a commitment and a calling. It is an experiment of faith and a living legacy. It is philosophically expansive and respectful of all cultures. It is vigorous and vigilant.

The desire for peace is natural in all people. When our minds are clear, we see the world inclusively instead of exclusively. Peace is an understanding at the cellular level that we are all connected. We know instinctively that we live better and more honorable lives when we don't arbitrarily try to sever that connection. We respect people and their traditions no matter how different they are from our own. When our minds are riddled with insecure thoughts, we operate from fear. And if fear is present, an enemy—real or imagined—can't be far behind.

Peace is our natural state of mind. War is the aberration.

We are all born with the birthright of a mind that is capable of pure clarity as well as total distraction—regardless of our intellectual capacity. We live our lives navigating the continuum between these two ends of the spectrum. The intuitive understanding of peace exists within our clear mind. We don't need to search outside ourselves for a way to create peace anymore than we search for ways to breathe. Because these functions are innate, they are invisible to us until they are compromised.

When we "come back to our senses" and truly set our sights on peace, we naturally look beyond what we might consider external "peaceful conditions." We don't make a list of things we don't want. We don't make a list of things we should be doing. We look inside ourselves to see what we are capable of being. We look outside ourselves to see how we can be of service to the well-being of others. We listen to the needs of others from their perspective instead of prescribing our favorite remedies. We don't withhold the lessons of science and technology based on greed. Respect and compassion are our autopilot. Our natural understanding of peace is the foundation that informs us who we are, what we can do, and how we can do it.

We are human beings and cannot live a life of perfection. We will get off track. We will have to learn we no longer have the luxury of indulging our prejudices. We can no longer assume we possess the one right way to view a circumstance or solve a problem. But, if our psychological compass is set toward peace, we will find our way back to the path of living a legacy we can be proud to leave to future generations, and one they will be grateful to receive.

Peace is indeed a privilege. Our responsibility is to preserve and protect it from the hubris of others—and more importantly, our own.

———◆———

Responsibility does not only lie with the leaders of our countries or with those who have been appointed or elected to do a job. It lies with each of us individually.

Dalai Lama

LIVE FOR YOUR COUNTRY

Off you go to another country
To be their unwelcome guest.
Off you go to lay your life down,
Then come home to be laid to rest.

Your country asks for a contribution.
It requires the ultimate test.
Be careful what you offer
When you give your ultimate best.

Is the best you give your country
A life you couldn't live?
Or would your country be better served
By the talents you could give?

Who is the greatest patriot,
The one who lives or the one who dies?
Should a nation require a young boy's death
To be seen as hero in its eyes?

What would you rather honor?
What would you rather give?
The bravery it takes to die,
Or the courage it takes to live?

KITCHEN TABLE

We come down the stairs
And take our mutual places.
We sit in comfy chairs
And say our mutual graces.

We bow our heads as we've been taught,
We fold our hands and pray.
We try some conversation,
We tell news of the day.

Food is passed around
The length of the kitchen table.
We pretend that life is normal
As much as we are able.

The pauses are a bit too long.
We can't meet each other's eyes.
We want the meal to be over.
That's how it is when someone dies.

We don't look at the empty chair.
Instead we just pretend
That our family's still intact,
Instead of at an end.

WHAT PRICE TRUCE

When a decision has been made,
When a time has been appointed,
When the papers have been signed,
When hands have been shaken,
When journalists have called their papers,
When photos have been taken,
When film is in the can,
When the press has aired the story,
When the world's been put on notice,
When families have been notified,

How can killing still continue?
How can destruction still be wrought?
How can people still be maimed?
How can infrastructure still be destroyed?
How can water still be polluted?
How can mines still be laid?
How can foxholes still be dug?
How can mortars still be launched?
How can grenades still be lobbed?
How can guns still be fired?
How can bayonets still be plunged?

When a truce is scheduled for midnight,
How can we kill until 11:59?

WE DECLARE

We can declare
That war is over,
And every act
Of war will cease.

But, we can only declare
The end of war.
We can't declare
The start of peace.

ENEMY FRIEND

I kneel here before you,
Your eyes filled with sorrow.
You can wound me, or kill me,
Or let me live 'til tomorrow.

Our lands are at war,
Yet we've never met.
And nothing you've done
Has made me upset.

I see that you're tired.
I'm bone weary too.
And I'm numb from the fear
That cuts us in two.

I offer my hand
And hope you'll take mine.
I stand up to face you
And straighten my spine.

I tell you my story
Knowing you can't understand.
I mean no harm or malice
To your people or land.

My brother, my keeper,
My savior, my friend.
Please spare and protect me
Don't let my life end.

I knew every smell,
I knew every sound.
I just didn't know
This was enemy ground.

I can see that you're thinking
About what to do.
My fate's in your hands,
And I must trust you.

Your eyes held your message,
Your decision about me.
It was an act of pure courage
When you set me free.

PEACE FULL

In a world full of hunger,
In a world full of pain,
The older and younger
Will live lives in vain.

In a world full of loving,
Man will find his release
In the courage to live
In a world filled with peace.

TIME IS OF THE ESSENCE

Time is of the essence,
Don't waste a single moment.
Fly life a little higher,
Soar love a little longer.

Be sure you know your purpose,
It makes life so much clearer.
Gently grasp your passion,
Hold it lightly, hold it nearer.

We have some finite hours,
We don't know their summation.
Put care into their substance,
Give them beauty and elation.

If peace is what you want,
Then peace is what you give.
If love is what you want,
Then love is what you live.

If you want to live upon this planet,
Be prepared to give it all its due.
Time is of the essence
In everything you do.

I LEARNED ABOUT LIVING

I learned about living
From a boy who was dying.
We shared in our giving
With both of us crying.

We tried to believe
He'd get a reprieve.
But his fate was leaving,
And my fate was grieving.

We made plans for great beauty
Which now are my duty.
I must be alive
For our dreams to survive.

He was a boy meant to dance,
To have love and romance.
But we both lost our chance
When death took its stance.

He said "Heaven's bells ring
When I hear you sing".
So his love of a song
Would send him along.

We knew from the start
We shared but one heart.
We became more than whole
When we merged our two souls.

It would soon be too late
For us to create.
So we dreamed of a way
For his spirit to stay.

We knew that our art
Grew deep in the heart.
We must quickly get started
Before he departed.

He said while I was young
There were songs to be sung.
And my later life's message
Would make use of war's presage.

He said I must use
His spirit as muse,
So projects could choose me
And all art forms could use me.

If I listen to him only
He'll guide me with care.
He'll give me new voice
For the message I'll share.

He said he'd be with me
In rooms and dark hallways.
I would see him in nature.
He'd be with me always.

The words that he spoke
Before his last breath,
Were words I could live by
Long after his death.

To know we can love
Is spiritually freeing.
The sharing of love
Is our purpose for being.

TIME SLOWLY PASSES

Time slowly passes
Like water poured from glasses.
And all the while,
The memory of your smile
Comes back to me
Gentle as a touch upon my knee.

Your voice was music to my ear.
Your picture brings a little tear.
Though one of us is older,
Your presence just gets bolder.
The thought of you brings back my youth,
And urges me to speak our truth.

I can speak, but can they hear?
Can they listen through their fear?
If they close their ears and shut their eyes,
They'll be deaf and blind to mortal cries.
I expected enemies to defy me,
I never guessed my country would deny me.

I look into my mirror.
I've tried to live with grace.
The signature of time
Is written on my face.
No matter how I try,
I can't forget that place.

All these years I've waited
For someone to say they cared.
And now I finally realize.
They're silent because they're scared.

OUR PURPOSE IS TO LOVE EACH OTHER

My face was blown apart from me,
It's not a pretty visage.
I used to be so handsome,
Now I only have an image.

My parts were disassembled,
I don't know how to gather them.
I have fantasies of wholeness,
Then my dreams come by to shatter them.

My legs have been misplaced somewhere,
I doubt that I can find them.
Only sockets where my eyes once were,
There's pain each time you bind them.

With so many missing bits of me,
It's so strange that I still live.
But, it's love that keeps me going,
And I've plenty still to give.

My family may not know my face,
But, my message should be freeing.
When I wrap them in a warm embrace,
And tell them how I'm feeling.

I'm not my missing pieces,
They're not my sole identity.
If my children donate love to the world,
I'll have been a worthy entity.

War promotes our separation.
Life's lesson draws us nearer.
Our purpose is to love each other,
Nothing could be clearer.

VIET NAM COUNSEL

Viet Nam as your counsel
Would say war's never done.
There's a legacy of atrocity
No matter who thinks they've "won".

The sad truths of war
Beg to be told
To prevent starting new ones
And learn from the old.

Open your eyes
Open your ears.
To hide from the shame
Won't quiet the fears.

Land mines still kill
After thirty odd years.
The wounded and maimed
Are left with their tears.

War begets war
As night follows day.
Blind eyes to consequences
Can't keep them away.

You believed your own lies
And the false hope it gave you.
Own up to your errors.
Silence can't save you.

Truth's not always easy
But tell it you must.
It's the only safe course
To regain global trust.

When sabers are rattled
The dangers increase.
It takes hubris to risk war.
It takes courage to risk peace.

THE RISK OF PEACE

The risk of peace is pricey.
It buries sacred cows.
It requires that we honor
Old-fashioned sacred vows.

If we take a chance on peace,
We run the risk of being wrong.
We see that in the brotherhood of humanity
We're not the only ones who belong.

We risk being seen as fallible.
We're not in total control.
We'd risk giving up our own opinion
To hear the wisdom of the whole.

We risk not having the final word.
We risk not exercising our might.
We risk the entire world knowing
We're not the arbiters of right.

If resources of the world are shared,
Global economy's abundant.
If we risk the choice of peace,
Then war becomes redundant.

A pledge to live in harmony
Is a quest that's never finished.
If we risk a world where peace prevails,
Humanity's not diminished.

If peace is our unwavering intention,
Battles of prejudice naturally cease.
War is the answer of the coward.
It requires courage to live in peace.

PEACE IS

Quiet and forceful.
Humble, respectful, compassionate, and resolute.
Courageous, strong, and resilient.
Vigorous, dynamic, and vital.
The mind of a child not yet contaminated by cynicism.
The smile in the eyes of a stranger.
An enemy who comforts you while you are dying.
The muscle of the heart versus the muscle of the fist.
Able to see its own flaws as well as those of others.
A thought more honorable than a deed.
A way of being that inspires what we do.
The willingness to silence the sounds of ego.
Equipped with a vibrant sense of humor.
Staying in the game when others fail to appear.
As bold as global action and
As humble as a simple thought.
Determined to avoid self-importance.
A desire for others to live in safety and well-being.
A willingness to sacrifice our wants for their needs.
Living in service to the greater good.
A state of mind.
Listening without expectations
About what we might hear.
Cloaked in hope and born of dreams.
The potential before the fact.
An experimental journey far more
Important than any imagined destination.
Words of kindness spoken in a language
We don't understand.

PRECIOUS PEACE

Oh, Precious Peace
You never have forsaken me.
All the while I was distracted
You always kept your gaze on me.

I kept trying to find my place,
Forgetting there was ample room
For all of us to live together
Without sacrifice or doom.

I forgot that you were present
From the moment of my birth.
I forgot you were present for all of us
Who populate this earth.

COURAGE

Courage isn't very special.
It's not about brains or who's stronger.
We all play tough games of life.
Some people just stay in them longer.

Courage is quiet,
No bluster or shout.
It's the strength from within
That conquers our doubt.

Courage is gentle
As it looks in your eyes.
It speaks to your soul
In whispers and sighs.

Courage is elusive.
You can't find it by searching.
Courage finds you
While your stomach is lurching.

Courage has beauty
And true depth of spirit.
It helps us through hardships
If we've just ears to hear it.

Courage can't make us immune
From adversity and woes.
It can't guarantee
We'll vanquish all foes.

Courage embraces our fears,
Yet it's not a pretender.
It can't always win;
It just doesn't surrender.

GOING BACK AGAIN

I come back to you alone,
As I did so long ago.
The fact that we would meet again
Is something we couldn't know.

You tried to kill me twice you know.
Will you try to make it three?
You tried to hold me captive
When I wanted to be free.

There was a time I feared you.
I didn't know your land's intent
Until I had time's distance
To see you reinvent.

There was a time we lived in terror,
Each afraid of the other's knife.
Let's set aside what we once were
And commit to peaceful life.

There are some things I left here.
Some things I'd really like to find.
I noticed when I got back home,
My youth and heart were left behind.

I learned so much of life from you,
A part of me will always stay.
I'll hold you in my heart
And think of you each day.

I come to you in friendship.
I have a big request;
To live in peaceful coexistence
And put demons to their rest.

I admire your courage and your stamina.
I know what you've been through.
It's not easy when you're oppressed
To create a life that's new.

I come to you alone again,
Much like I did before.
It's time for us to reunite
In a time that isn't war.

COULD YOU REALLY HAVE A WAR?

If you saw humanity in others,
Could you really have a war?
If no one was willing to fight
You'd have to close the door.

If you saw others as your brothers,
If you were interested in their customs,
If you could see your common ground,
If you thought of them as friends,
If you weren't concerned with being "right",
If you didn't feel the need to judge,
If you wanted to give and share instead of take,
If you had tolerance and patience,
If you had faith, hope, charity, and love,
If you knew that they did too,
If you could see life through their eyes,
If you saw connection instead of fearing difference,
If you didn't see through the eyes of good and bad,
If you didn't need to impose your views on others,
If you valued their lives as much as yours,
If you exercised love instead of hatred.
If you understood we're all just versions of each other,
Could you really have a war?

CONSTANT SPIRIT

It takes a constant spirit
To serve in turbulent times,
To subdue the foe of fear,
To heal the turbulent mind.

It takes a constant spirit
To silence the voice of doubt,
To tame the haunted memory,
To embrace what life's about.

It takes a constant spirit
To live as loyal friend,
To be physician to the psyche
So souls and hearts can mend.

It takes a constant spirit
To give meaning to life's flame,
To live in service to humanity,
To do honor to one's name.

WHAT WAS YOUR INTENTION

You didn't intend to cause another's pain,
But did you intend to cause them comfort?

You didn't intend to frighten him,
But did you intend to create safety and security?

You didn't intend to cut her off,
But did you intend to give her room?

You didn't intend to stifle their curiosity,
But did you intend to help them grow?

You didn't intend to be rude,
But did you intend to be respectful?

You didn't intend to tell a lie,
But did you intend to tell the truth?

You didn't intend to create distance,
But did you intend to establish connection?

You didn't intend to make an enemy,
But did you intend to make a friend?

You didn't intend to hurt my feelings,
But did you intend to love me?

You didn't intend to suffocate the spirit of the world,
But did you intend to uplift humanity?

You didn't intend to wage a war,
But did you intend to wage peace?

ONE AMONG THE MANY

We are single drops of water.
We are single grains of sand.
Together we fill the ocean,
And create desert on the land.

Waves rise and fall.
Tides ebb and flow.
Where the sands will shift tomorrow,
It's unlikely we'll know.

These are powerful forces of nature.
Human nature's a similar force.
We're raw energy on the move.
The challenge is to stay on course.

It takes all the grains and all the drops
To create the land and ocean.
No one is more important than the other
To keep the earth in motion.

People are like the grains and drops.
We each have an essential job to do.
None of us is extraneous.
Life requires all of me and all of you.

We're sculpted from the same human clay,
Just wanting to be understood.
We're an ancient, primitive sculpture
Carved from a single piece of wood.

We are never single islands.
We are dependent on each other.
We are linked in eternal purpose.
We are each other's brother.

No act is done in isolation.
We have the privilege to stand in unity.
What's done to one is done to many.
We must create a world community.

GIVE MY LOVE TO THE WORLD

Give my heart to my mother,
Since she gave it life.

Give my courage to my father,
So he can carry on.

Give my knowledge to my sister,
To help her learn of life.

Give my faith to my brother,
To help him feel secure.

Give my hope to my friends,
To help them build a future.

Give my love to the world,
In thanks for my time here.

EMBARKING ON
THE PATH OF PEACE

The path of peace begins not with what we want to tell others, but what we ask of ourselves.

Penny Rock

EMBARKING ON THE PATH OF PEACE

How do we embark on the path of peace? How do we locate it? How do we begin the journey? Notice I said path "of," not "to." Peace is not a place we go; it is a state of mind we come from. Locating the path is simple. It's inside us individually and gains strength and momentum when understood and experienced collectively. I don't mean staging or joining rallies and marches. Peace is not an event. It is a solitary thought in a solitary mind that moves a solitary heart.

If activities in the *name* of peace emanate from the arrogant judgment of those who believe peace is not possible and that there is a need for a national position of supremacy, it is not born of the *spirit* of peace. It will be peppered by speeches *at* people instead of listening *to* people. If that happens, how are we different from those whose philosophies and ideologies we find oppressive? We have a responsibility to offer hope, to help people see their role in living in a respectful and peaceful society.

No matter what costume ego wears, the armor of war or the flowers of peace, it never serves the public good. Events that spring from ego may excite, but they will never inspire.

Where the Path Begins

The path of peace begins not with what we want to *tell others*, but what we *ask of ourselves*. Peace is not about engaging in a flurry of good deeds. It is about engaging in clear-minded personal reflection. When we ask *ourselves* questions about what our vision of peaceful living includes, we become inspired. Insights that bubble up from inspiration are always in service of the greater good, are always inclusive rather than exclusive, and automatically evolve into wise, common sense, focused action. And those actions may include rallies, marches, and deeds. The magnetic pull of a shared vision takes on a different tone when ignited by inspiration, vision, and compassion rather than fueled by fear, anger, and judgment. Whenever inspiration and vision are in the driver's seat, focused action will begin.

Once we have envisioned what it means to live as peaceful global citizens, we can ask ourselves questions with practical and profound implications such as:

- Do our daily actions represent our vision of peace?
- Does our educational system represent that vision?
- Do we teach our children how to live as contributors *to* instead of consumers *of* what a peaceful society offers?
- Do we treat and respect our planet as the gracious host it is?
- Do we value the life and well-being of others as much as our own?

- Do we ask those we elect to preserve the public trust in their positions and plans for peace without settling for platitudes and policies?

- Do we understand peace cannot be legislated?

- Do we expect our government to have cabinet-level focus and strategy about peace that guides our domestic and foreign policy?

- Do we understand that *each* of us is a member of "We the People?"

A life devoted to peace is not exempt from conflict. However, the approach to resolution is significantly different. It is predicated on staying engaged and knowing a common understanding is possible. We will still review our history to learn what it can teach us about our present and future. The creative arts will continue to draw our attention to that which is the best *and* the worst in our human condition. Our history and our art are voices of our collective conscience. The choice to listen or ignore is ours, and ours alone.

Ordinary People with Big Dreams Produce Extraordinary Results

Peace is a right of every ordinary human being on the planet. There are no special requirements or credentials because there are no special people.

I write this because it is on my mind in my daily life, but I am not a paragon of virtue. I am as flawed and opinionated as the next person. I am one of those ordinary people. I just don't want to lose my grasp on the dream and vision. I don't want to dilute it. If *I* don't reflect on it, how can I recommend that others do so? And if *we* don't reflect on it and act on it, individually and collectively, nothing will happen. We can't wait for "other" people to take the first step. There is no quorum for peace. Even in a march of millions, we each must take our own single steps.

I am not advocating the simple exchange of sweet sentiments. I think we need dynamic dialogue to hold our feet to the fire and put our money where our mouths are. We need to uncap the wells of hope. Without hope there are no dreams. Big actions don't take place without big dreams. I think we dream too small, and that never serves humanity. Without dreams nothing happens. No creation. No invention. No discovery.

Our lives depend on how big we are able to dream. Future generations will be expanded or limited by the size and clarity of our dreams. And sometimes we will fail. So what? Failure always comes right before success. So who are we to say when it's time to quit dreaming? Who are we to say when it's time to stop taking action? Who are we to indulge our arrogant defeatism at the expense of the welfare of future generations?

How can we spend more time and money devising more efficient mechanisms of war? How can we spend more time and money on devising more economical means to kill, maim and torture? How can we spend no time in national dialogue devising a strategy for peace that demonstrates the human and economic benefits for our national *and* global society?

Sometimes I feel daunted when I think these thoughts and say these words. They're bigger than I am. I can't snap my fingers and change the world. Nor should I be able to do so because finding a way to live together peacefully is a collective enterprise. And living together peacefully requires perspective and a sense of humor. If we can't see our own pitfalls, we will stumble more often and over bigger bumps. Without the ability to see our own responsibilities and our own flaws and errors, we become the embodiment of the kind of arrogance we say we deplore. We risk alienating those who may be open to engaging in dialogue about the possibility of a society that is healthier for all its citizens.

Living peacefully means we keep our eyes on and engage in creating the bigger picture. But the picture is made up of the millions of brush strokes of who we are and what we do in our daily lives.

We have only moments in the hourglass of life on this earth. How better can we spend those moments than to live the legacy we wish to leave?

———————◆———————

If you can't feed a hundred people, then feed just one.

Mother Teresa

ELIGIBILITY TO VOTE

The Twenty-Sixth Amendment to the United States Constitution lowered the eligible age to vote from twenty-one to eighteen. It was adopted July 1, 1971. The amendment was the result of student activism against the Vietnam War and the inability to express their views in the voting booth about being conscripted to fight. President Eisenhower was the first president to publicly state his support for suffrage for those eighteen and older. The slogan "Old enough to fight, old enough to vote," dated back to WWII when President Roosevelt reduced the military draft age to eighteen.

PRODUCTS AND SERVICES

Products
Books:
We Declare: The Truth About War and Our
　　Responsibility for Peace

He Called Me Lieutenant Angel: A Love Song From War

Power of a Clear Mind: The Direct Link Between Your
　　Leadership State of Mind, The Decisions You Make,
　　The Actions You Take, The Results You Get

Audio CDs:
Power of a Clear Mind: Keep Your Bearings in *Any*
　　Circumstance

The 8 Essential Ingredients of Healing: From *Anything,*
　　Anywhere, Anytime

Services
Executive Consulting & Coaching: Individual and
　　Executive Teams

Transfer of Competency: Workshops for Consultants
　　and Coaches

Speaker: Key-Note and Conference Speaker

Learn More
To order or to learn more about Penny's Products and
　　Services, visit: www.powerofaclearmind.com

Penny may be contacted directly at:
　　penny@powerofaclearmind.com

ABOUT THE AUTHOR

Penny Rock is an Executive Consultant and Coach, Vietnam War Veteran, Breast Cancer Survivor, Inspirational Speaker, and Author.

Penny is the author of the books, *He Called Me Lieutenant Angel: A Love Song from War, We Declare: The Truth About War and Our Responsibility for Peace*, and *Power of a Clear Mind: The Direct Link Between Your Leadership State of Mind, the Decisions You Make, The Actions You Take, The Results You Get*. She has recorded the audio CDs, *Power of a Clear Mind*, and *The 8 Essential Ingredients of Healing*.

Penny was featured in the Academy Award nominated documentary film, *A Healing*, and was the inspiration for Normi Noel's play, *No Background Music*, originally produced at Shakespeare & Company in August 2006. *No Background Music* was adapted for BBC World Wide Radio, premiered in September 2005, and won the Sony Gold Drama award in 2006. Penny is portrayed by Sigourney Weaver.

www.ingramcontent.com/pod-product-compliance
Lightning Source LLC
Chambersburg PA
CBHW050542280326
41933CB00011B/1682